I0436891

In The Eye Of The Storm

SURVIVING THE AFTERMATH

STEVEN M. BANKA

Bloomington, IN  Milton Keynes, UK

authorHOUSE®

AuthorHouse™
1663 Liberty Drive, Suite 200
Bloomington, IN 47403
www.authorhouse.com
Phone: 1-800-839-8640

AuthorHouse™ *UK Ltd.*
500 Avebury Boulevard
Central Milton Keynes, MK9 2BE
www.authorhouse.co.uk
Phone: 08001974150

*This book is a work of non-fiction. Unless otherwise noted, the author
and the publisher make no explicit guarantees as to the accuracy of
the information contained in this book and in some cases, names
of people and places have been altered to protect their privacy.*

First published by AuthorHouse 7/26/2006

ISBN: 1-4259-4876-6 (sc)

*Printed in the United States of America
Bloomington, Indiana*

This book is printed on acid-free paper.

In this epic story of what one man saw, we explore his survival of the storm, hurricane Katrina. The hurricane had wind gusts of up to 165 miles per hour in most parts of southeast Louisiana. However, hurricane Katrina isn't the storm this story talks about, but the storm after the hurricane. The story takes place in New Orleans, the Big Easy. The city is turned upside down with looting, fires, rapes, kidnapping, gun fire, killings, stabbings, fighting and explosions. With every chapter thinking it's at it's worst, it gets even worse. How one man can survive is told in this story.

"I wouldn't want my worst enemy to endure what I went through."

Steven Banka

CONTENTS

Chapter One	WATCHING THE STORM	1
Chapter Two	THE HURRICANE AT DAWN	5
Chapter Three	THE DAY AFTER	9
Chapter Four	DECISION OF SURVIVAL	15
Chapter Five	SURVIVAL OF THE FITTEST	19
Chapter Six	DAWN OF THE DEAD	23
Chapter Seven	KILL OR BE KILLED	27
Chapter Eight	FIRE IN THE SKY	31
Chapter Nine	BACK AT IT AGAIN	35
Chapter Ten	DAY OF REJOICE	41
Chapter Eleven	THE LONG RIDE	43
Chapter Twelve	A BASE IN RUIN	45
Chapter Thirteen	HELPING HANDS	47
Acknowledgments		51

CHAPTER ONE

Watching the Storm

Our story begins in New Orleans, Louisiana. 43 hours before landfall of hurricane Katrina at or around the mouth of the Mississippi river, New Orleans is calm and not expecting the hurricane to hit directly. The Mississippi river is a major trade port with many barges up and down the river.

I'm at lunch watching the president on the news urging New Orleanians to leave and seek higher ground. "Yeah right, just like last year, it'll turn at the last second." I said as I watch the news bulletin. The whole morning seemed normal and no one was thinking about evacuating New Orleans. "There is an easterly wind coming off Mexico and will push the hurricane towards Mississippi." I said as if I were a meteorologist. Little did I know the hurricane was growing rapidly. The stronger the hurricane, the bigger the surge. I thought we were protected by floodgates, why should we run? So the joke of the day was, "Are you running or staying?" If I would have known what I know now, I would be packing my bags. All my co-workers that I asked seemed to be staying. Everything was normal so far, and I was writing down next weeks schedule. After lunch I get back to work and even till the end of the day, everything was calm and no one was in a rush to evacuate.

I live with a roommate, her brother and our friend Chris. I asked my roommate and her brother what their plans were when I got home. They wanted to stay with their family. Chris said his family left but he wanted to stay with us, because we all lived together at the time. That's what family does, stick together till the end. Later that night we watched the storm build up to a category 5 hurricane. That's when everyone who could afford to leave started to leave New Orleans. I know I didn't have $100 to just up and leave for a few days. So I stayed and waited for the storm expecting to hit in 36 hours.

The next morning I awoke to news that New Orleans was under a mandatory evacuation. Now the hurricane is expected to hit in 24 hours. Looking at the T.V. screen you see gridlock evacuation to the east. "The east, why not go west to Baton Rouge and then north to Arkansas." Everyone leaving in the same direction stuck for hours. Like in "Day After Tomorrow" and the water rushed in the city. I thought, "It's not going to be that bad." Then I found out that New Orleans is shut down and everyone is told to evacuate. At least I get a day off out of all this.

Who would have thought about not coming back to New Orleans at this point? No one, not even me.

The day went on normal as can be, no sudden preparations. Then my roommate gets a ride to go look for batteries and candles. So we ride around a city in panic. Gas stations closed or sold out, except for one Spur station. Hardware stores closed, the local grocer sold out of most survival essentials. "Man this is mad crazy, people are really over reacting because of what the mayor says." Keep in mind every hurricane missed us, or was just rain and wind. So we went home to see what we had in case the electric went out. All we had was a few candles, water in the fridge and in the tub to flush with. This is the most I've prepared for a hurricane, the others never hit.

The rest of the day everyone mentally prepared for the hurricane by praying every 3 hours, praying for God to protect us. As night fall came, the hurricane is expected to hit in 10 hours, we prayed for some rest. Little did we know we wouldn't rest for the next week.

CHAPTER TWO

The Hurricane at Dawn

I awoke to the sound of rain and a little thunder. It's about 7 in the morning and I got little sleep that night, worrying about the hurricane. Winds were gusting at approximately 25 miles per hour around 7:30 a.m. I am the type of person to go out into the storm, look it in the face, and laugh. So I did. I look outside to a cloudy sky raining like a shower that never stops. Awaiting for the real gusts of wind, I travel quietly throughout the house to see who's up. See we live in a shotgun house, meaning that there aren't separate rooms. You have to actually travel through someone's room to get to the bathroom or kitchen. It goes living room to an open room bedroom, meaning no wall. You travel to the other bedroom next, then bathroom, dining room and then kitchen to the back yard. So I have to travel through the other rooms where my friends are sleeping to get outside. My roommate's brother and Chris are knocked out sleep through the rain. I guess rain makes you tired. My roommate is up and looking at me like I'm crazy and that I shouldn't go outside. I'm excited to be in wind that can take this house apart. Crazy, no I wouldn't call me crazy, just retarded. I should have been a storm tracker, I would love to watch tornadoes. I knew we were going to get hit by the left side of the hurricane, and that it would turn enough for the eye to miss us. When the winds picked up about 80 miles per hour I went outside indeed. I was acting like M.J. in the Bad video with my shirt open hollering OAH!! Then a gust of wind pushed me back 3 steps and that's when I knew I should go in. Not to mention that stop sign just flew past my head, but hey I'm ok. If a board from off a house would have come toward me I knew I was going to get hit, so I went back in. In the kitchen the roof sounded like it was tearing off and the boards were hitting the ceiling.

Around 9a.m. the gusts seem to be getting up to approximately 100 miles per hour, especially in the alley. I had to go outside in that wind to nail the shutter to the house. I stood outside holding the shutter, but I couldn't nail it because of the wind. My roommate nailed it shut. The rain is freezing and the wind is no help at all. Then I heard a loud BOOM, the electric box for the block had just exploded. On the next block a huge tree fell over and is laying across the block.

By 12p.m. water is finally gotten all across the street. Winds have died down a little, but at a higher elevation winds were bending trees in half. We steadily watch the water as it rises because the power went out and the candles were lit. The day goes on and we wait to see if it'll ever stop raining.

Something seems odd because the water is up to the curb at 3p.m. To me it is oddly rising, but it may just be the rain. Chris decided to go up the street by the downed tree to see it up close, so I went with him. As we got to the end of the block by the tree we saw an elderly woman who was worried about the water rising into her house. We didn't know if it would ever stop, so we told the woman that we would come back to check on her if it got worse. As we got back to the house, we noticed that my roommate was hunting for batteries or even a flashlight. Everyone is wondering where the cell phone with the radio is. I forgot to get batteries and let alone get a 9v battery for the flash light. As my roommate puts on the radio she finds out that the 17th street canal and the industrial canal had broken. We look at the water rising, now realizing we don't know when it'll stop. We try to stop the water from getting into the front door, then we find out how durable the floors are. Water is coming in through the bottom, now I know to put everything up way high. As the water comes in the house, we begin to pray again. The 3 o'clock prayer in hopes that the water will stop.

Then we worry about the houses in the 9th ward. I'm glad my daughters left a week ago, because their grandmother's house is off of St. Maurice and Galvez. I'm sure it's gone, with a barge breaking the levee over there, nothing can survive it's path. What was a barge doing in the industrial canal anyway?

As night falls the water is still rising and we see stars. We never see this many stars in New Orleans. Power is gone everywhere except the French Quarter. That's when you know it's really serious. Something like this has never happened in like 40 years. Then as we see the water still rising at a rate of ¾ inch an hour, we start worrying about those who can't swim, especially my roommates' mother. My roommate starts to panic because there is no communication with her. She stays in the 7th ward by St. Bernard which is closer to the levee that broke. So we start thinking that they have more water than we do. Everyone starts freaking out, I need a drink. Sleep is not an option because there is no floor to sleep on. My bed is floating and the air mattress is the only option we have for getting out. My roommate can't swim either, but she is small enough to fit on it. Would you call it losing faith because we didn't get what we prayed for? I don't think so, everything happens for a reason. We shouldn't panic about 8ft of water everywhere we look. We just lose our minds, we never experienced this kind of emergency. The rain is over but the lake is about 3-5 ft over full. That's a lot of water, it has to go somewhere, HERE!!! We try to play dominoes and some blackjack to get the water off our minds. We look at the walls and measure where the water was an hour ago. Will it ever stop?

CHAPTER THREE

The Day After

Hoping that the liquor and the games would get the water off our minds, we aren't very tired. The guys try to be as quiet as can be because my roommate had finally fallen asleep. As for us, we only get about an hour of sleep at best. "Dominoe, let's play again." At about 5 in the morning we started to pack essential needs. I didn't pack anything because I have been in this predicament before in my life. Survival mode kicked in for me, seeing my backyard full of water started it all. I then realized I had to go out into it. If I didn't, I would have to risk the chance of going to the roof and getting ate up by mosquitoes. I grab the axe and a sheet of plywood and head to the attic, which was next door. I had to go into the backyard, swim to the other backdoor, and make my way up a thin ladder. I slid the sheetrock up the ladder and placed it on the boards on the roof. I get ready to swing the axe upward, then I hear my roommate yelling for me. Everyone had decided to go out into the water and swim, because they don't know if their mom is ok.

They packed what they needed and I got the air mattresses together. The water is freezing outside at 6am, the crack of dawn. My phone got water damage as soon as the water rose to reach the truck battery. The car alarm kept going off and the alarm switch got water damage. I had to then disconnect the power to the battery, dangerous enough while wading waist high in water. I wanted to come back and get stuff like the Playstation 2, my stereo, a couple pictures and a T.V. so I put everything up high to come back to. We waited until we could see what was in the water, which was about 7:30 a.m. tired as can be and fighting water. "My legs are going to get a good workout in this water." We heard about the barge that broke the industrial canal, and that they could see the dead bodies floating in the water from the helicopter. We had one helicopter that was going all over the city to witness the water damage. He went as far east as the NASA building and as far west as St. Rose, La. We thought the dead bodies would make their way to our area noticing that the water was coming toward us the whole time. By the time we got everything together, I just jumped into the water. I could have dove into a car part, a boat, a basket or anything else you could imagine. Yeah I'm retarded.

As we get ready to get into this freezing water, I wanted to test the air mattress. So I told my roommate to get on to see if it would float. It did indeed and there were two, so her brother got on the other one. Chris and I had to swim in most spots to get to higher ground. Of course Canal St. was in the median, the high point in the area. I used to work construction so I paid attention to the flow of water. I went in the opposite direction of flow to get to higher ground. As we head for Canal St. we hear yells and cries for help blocks away. "We can only help one person at a time. This isn't going to work, we need to find a better way to at least transport some of these people. We get to an abandoned office building and break the door to find a way to the roof. We heard that the helicopters were picking up the refugees and taking them to the superdome. Chris and I head back to go get others and bring them to the office building. After all they are our neighbors. As we head back we find a boat that was turned upside down. We thought there must be another one around here. Sure enough Chris and some other guys got together to get the boat. Rescue mission under way.

As we take the boat and the air mattresses to the people that can't swim or are too short, more and more yells are heard. So we split up, by 12p.m. we had approximately 70 people at the office building, next thing, food and water. Most people were breaking into the local corner store to get needs. I don't understand what need of alcohol is in most cases, but we all deal with this tragedy in our own way. We must had made about 7-10 trips back and forth with the boat and the air mattresses. At this point my roommate was really worried about her family. So I got Chris on his last trip and asked him if he wanted to go with me upstream to go see about my roommates' family. So we went ahead on this little journey. Rescue mission 2, as I recall we called it.

We made way up Canal St. to Galvez St. to get to St. Bernard. As we get past the Lafitte prodjects, we notice hundreds of people that couldn't escape the wraith of hurricane Katrina. The police had an airboat to survey how many people actually had to evacuate. Someone actually had a boat on Orleans Ave. Orleans is known for the Indians of Mardi Gras and the Grand Party at Claiborne Ave. You see it all on Orleans, and I have definitely seen it all now. A boat full of people, heading for the Superdome. The water was up to our necks at this point, so that would be about 6 ft of water. As we go further up Galvez though, the water seemed to be going down. By the time we get to Esplanade Ave. the water is only ankle deep. Makes you wonder for a second, Why is the high class water so low? Over here, people are driving through the water and making way to the I-10. Little do they know that Claiborne has about 4 ft. of water itself. As I look at the I-10 I see a couple of buses picking up people. By the time we get to St. Bernard the water is only about 4ft. deep. Nothing to worry about at all.

As we get to the house on Onzaga St. everyone seems to be fine. My roommates' people are cooking lunch and that they are doing fine. We stop our journey for a bite to eat and some water. I know I'm getting baked out there, especially with the heat bouncing off the water. Like when you go fishing, you need sunscreen. Everyone seems fine, my roommates' uncle was cracking jokes about how all this fell apart. We let my roommates' people know that we are going back to get them and that we'll be back about 6p.m. We arrived at the house about 2p.m. so we know it'll be another 2 hours to get there and 2 hours to get back. Believe me when I say that wading in water with a current takes a lot out of you. Rescue mission 3, laughing jokingly.

We get back to Galvez St. to get back down to Canal St. At this point Canal St. was really looking like a canal. Worried about food and water for my roommates, Chris and I go into the other corner store to get water. As we get back to the office building, we try not to smile, but can't help to give them the good news with a smile. That's when they knew everything was ok and that they needed not worry. At this point, my feet hadn't seen dry land in 5 hours, since being on the roof of the office building. I tried flagging down helicopters but there must had been more less fortunate people that needed rescuing. We need to go now, before we really get tired.

We head back up Galvez, this time with the air mattresses, which slows us up a bit. Everyone seems amazed at how many people are actually still in New Orleans. I see some faces I recognize and a lot of children that seem to be stranded. We left the boat back with the people at the office building. As we get to Onzaga St. you can feel the intensity of people rejoicing after worrying if they are ok. Everyone stays strong and no tears are shed, no time for that now. We still have about 4ft of water in front of us.

Everyone eats and everything seems to be ok for now. No one has made a final decision on evacuating, just to see if the water will go down. They have a battery powered T.V. that is broadcasting the helicopter flying all over the water flooded city. As we see that the French Quarter is only half wet, we start to consider leaving. It wasn't until they said that the water may rise again, and that the gas and water went out, that we realize it's time to go. At this time it's night and no light what so ever. Night watch is in effect. As I look up the street I see looters breaking into houses with shotguns at hand. I won't bother them as long as they don't bother me. I keep a watch out for the house as I sit across the street. Someone decides to flash a light into the house, and I get ready to jump into the water. He doesn't see me, and at the same time, uncle ran outside with the gun and ran him off. You hear gunshots in the distance and helicopters non stop flying overhead. If you are not on your roof, the helicopter will not pick you up. The night is restless.

CHAPTER FOUR

Decision of Survival

As the reports of the water coming our way get confirmed, we start packing our essentials. Chris found another boat, and I get woke to help him get it. When you have 4 people that can't swim it does help to have a boat. That's when we knew it's time to go. The news is reporting everyone to evacuate to the Convention Center because the Superdome is over packed and is severely damaged. They ask everyone to pack 1 bag each, so we do and then head out to the I-10. The quickest way should be above ground, we thought. As we get to the I-10, whose going to carry all these bags. I had to find a basket some kind of way. At this point Chris is worried about his family and seems to be on a rescue mission of his own. We split up and I looked for a basket with my roommates' brother. They try to tell us to take a boat, but how are we going to lift the basket out of the water. Metal sinks in water fast, it is too heavy to pick up into a boat. When we get back to the I-10 by everyone else we are not aware of what day it is nor what date, we just want to survive. We get first glance at how many people are actually still in the city. Trucks, semi's, buses are full of people coming from the eastern parts of New Orleans. The I-10 is full of water at Morrison Ave. and everyone that can get to the I-10 has to wait. People are speeding back and forth to get those who need to get to higher ground. Word has it that the surge alone destroyed the I-10 over the Lake Pontchartrain. We load up the two baskets and head for a long journey on the I-10 to get to the convention center. As we get to the next exit, we see fire trucks lined up on the other side. "There's a sniper!", yells the N.O.P.D. officer. There must have been 50 officers working on figuring out where this sniper was. There were 5 special ops with sniper rifles trying to scope him out. At about an hour later, they caught him. "Why would anyone be shooting people at a time like this!?!?" exclaimed my roommates' mother.

Each exit seemed like a mile apart. The whole journey must have been a 3 mile journey. We see people stealing the Ice-cream trucks to get cool and have transportation. As we get closer to the convention center, we notice there is no food or water. I thought maybe it was inside.

Police were no where to be found as we get inside the convention center. Everyone seems to be settling in, finding ways to cook food, ways to get comfortable and ways to mark territory. Everyone is waiting for the buses to arrive and get out of this hell. When we get inside the convention center, my roommates' mom finds her brother and his family. We made a decision that at a time like this we all need to stick together. Too many people inside one place, something is bound to happen. I suggested to go outside and be ready for the buses, that way when they do come we can be first in line. So I drag some chairs outside so we can sit on something.

This man seemed drunk and was mad about the situation of me dragging the chairs. He was blaming the white people and started to look at me. He get's mad and says, "Drag that f-ing chair some more and watch what I'll do." I slammed the chair, turned around, balled up my fist and my roommates' uncle pulled me back. When I tell you all the men gathered toward him, he backed off, but not without complaining about the situation. So we moved a few feet over to calm down.

As the sun went down so did our minds. With no police in sight, survival mode kicked in and I knew it was every man for himself. I've faced this before in the north while with a gang and also in jail. So this was nothing new to me, seeing 15 year old boys with butterfly knives in the bathroom. If I can survive the same situation in the north, I know I can survive this. An argument rages over a dominoe game. I watch them as they take it outside and then BANG! He shot and killed him over a dominoe game. I saw them not 5 minutes ago drinking Jack Daniels and playing dominoes. This is for real, I thought to myself. Wake up, can't fall asleep now. Wake up, I just kept talking to myself. Then the crowd says the buses are coming. Everyone is crowding the buses, trying to get away from the violence. The buses never stop, afraid that they may become the next victim. I understand that, what I don't understand is the fact that the Superdome is secure and we are not. Why not evacuate us in the day, when the violence is not high. Then at night evacuate the Superdome. Why? Why am I witnessing this trauma?

CHAPTER FIVE

Survival of the Fittest

Pitch black and there is no law, every man for himself. People really getting uncomfortable with the situation at hand. We made a spot for ourselves in front of the convention center and made sure that no one came in. Everyone tried to lay on the hard concrete to get some rest. A few moments later someone said that they were kidnapping the young children. No one knew whether to believe it or not, but I'm the type of person to investigate the matter. As the night rages on, so do the screams. A man in the park across the street hollering, "Get off me! Get …" then silence. In the morning we found the dead body in the grass.

Wednesday, the morning sun brings questions, confusion and trauma as the screams from the night before still linger in my head. Some people in the crowd say that the police want the elderly to come to the front of the convention center by the casino. Most of the elderly are dehydrated, left to die. I've seen 3 bodies already of the elderly here, dead. Have to look for water, so at the crack of dawn I hunt for water. I see people looting the corner stores for whatever is in there, but no one is touching the water supply. I get the water back to the crew that never knew I left. I let them know that we have to survive out here and that someone has to go get supplies.

The day goes on, all is quiet and we still here that the buses are coming. Where are they? The stench from the bathroom is overcoming the air that we breath. I go upstairs to the second floor to try to find if there is food in the refrigerators. The second floor stinks of crack cocaine and I try to find the stairs up as quickly as possible. I get to the third floor to find someone blocking an entrance to one of the meeting rooms. He is standing with a loaded oozi. I just keep going, I find a room with a freezer but something stinks. Someone yells, "Don't open that freezer, the odors from the dead bodies is terrible." I smelled it, but to actually see the bodies, I don't think I could handle that. I've seen dead bodies before and know what they smell like. Rumors said that the body count was at 22. No wonder everyone is outside instead of inside. I walk back downstairs and head towards the back of the convention center. I look for a freezer for something other than water to drink. The only thing left is a case of diet pepsi, I'll drink that and I know they will too. In this situation you don't ask questions because you don't know who is out to kill you. When you fear your own life is in danger, you don't go ask death for trouble. So I left well enough alone.

Watching your back 24/7 you tend to doze off in periods of about 30 minutes to an hour. As the night came you knew what might happen and you didn't want it to happen to you. The night was long, dark, funky, hard and most of all scary. Not knowing what would happen next you can't help be prepared. This is truly a movie, we all thought we would wake up and all this would be over. Not going to happen. Now we realize it wasn't the hurricane to fear, but the aftermath it brings.

CHAPTER SIX
Dawn of the Dead

As thousands of New Orleanians wake up to the living hell they are enduring, people see bodies in the distance. People are getting stabbed and there is no one here to protect us. Thursday and all is not well. Chaos rang out as someone broke into a corner store. Where is everyone going, I thought to myself. Curios Steve off to find out the unknown, seems they were running to be the first to get food and water. Even though most people were coming back with liquor. Amazingly the water was still there and no one wanted that. What are these people thinking about, alcohol will just dehydrate them and then what? Die of course, I don't want to die. I came back with the water and realized that our clothes were stinking. We hadn't changed clothes or took a bath in 4 days. Even after wading in that awful water and the sun drying the clothes didn't help.

I journey down the streets and watch as police try to patrol the area outside the convention center. They say not to go 2 blocks past the convention center in any direction. They had trucks and were loaded with double barrel pump shotguns. I made my way to a corner store that sold white t-shirts. I grabbed every size I could and then counted to make sure everyone had a change of clothes. Then I found a box of juices, so I grabbed them and made way back to the convention center. I had to watch my back in case the police were around. As I head back I keep getting the same response, "Can I have a juice?" or "Where you got that from?". The best one was, "I'll buy a juice from you." What am I going to do with money right now. There are no stores open for business and there is no way of transportation to get around. I looked at him like he was crazy and responded with, "This is for the kids." I was surrounded by 20 kids wanting 12 juices and they were outside our family. So I gave out the juices accordingly and made sure every kid in our group got a juice. I really didn't want to drink anything at this point. The question running through my mind was, Am I going to live to see tomorrow? Everyone seemed a little worried as to where I was. I told them that no matter what time it is, I still have to risk my life to get the stuff WE need to survive. Sorry I didn't let you know, but first come, first serve.

Chris wanted to see what was left of this city. So we left again, only to see a city in havoc and seeing that everyone was trying to escape. After the cries in the night, everyone seemed to want to get away from this horror. They tried to steal every car they could. Only to find out the only way out was by Airline Hwy and they had a patrol of police waiting for those who stole cars. Why are you worried about arresting people? Are we in a third world country now? Is this what is more important now, instead of food and water? This is ridiculous.

Walking up the street we see looters taking everything they can get their hands on. How are they going to get a flat screen T.V. on a bus? Even when the military is checking everything you have. They are going to let you know not to have alcohol, guns and especially no stolen goods. We are under martial law, which means they have the right to shoot to kill. The thought of looting crossed my mind until a pump sawed off shotgun was in my face.

CHAPTER SEVEN
Kill or Be Killed

As I enter the riverwalk for food or water at the food court entrance, no police or army are to be found. I turn the corner and 3 people in casual clothes ask, "What do you want here? There is nothing to see here so turn around and go back out the way you came in!" So I ask, "Who are you?" They responded, "We are the New Orleans Police Department, now if you don't leave we will shoot you." So I ask, "What are you doing for food and water for the people at the convention center?" They responded, "We don't know what is going on as far as food and water, but you need to go back to the convention center and stay OUT of the Riverwalk" Seeing a pump in your face your train of thought tends to go more towards survival. I was thinking about a way to escape, trying to take the gun if it were necessary, what to do in this situation and most of all am I about to die. All they could tell me is that they don't know what is going on and that they have the right to shoot to kill.

Are we refugee-civilians or are we suicide bombers? Are we American citizens or people from another country with the intent to kill? Are we innocent people trying to escape or wild animals in a herd? This is not how you treat people that need to be evacuated. Where is FEMA? Are they not supposed to help those in a time of need? Sure all hell breaks loose at night, what do you expect when you don't have police patrolling at night. Is the Superdome not a secure area where people can't stampede to get on a bus? Then why not evacuate them at night, and patrol the convention center at night? Most of all, where was the food and water? Why point fingers, why not take control of a situation that is out of control?

I walk back to the group asking myself these questions. As soon as I get to the last question, I see an Regional Transit Authority bus packed with about 60 people in it heading for Baton Rouge. The RTA is the local bus line for the city of New Orleans. The one I saw was in fact stolen to get away from this hell. Why didn't anyone think to get these buses to the prodjects at least, to evacuate people to safety. People can't afford to just up and leave, we do live check by check because of higher cost of living. Then you see another RTA bus that was stolen full of people that were at the convention center. How in the world did the RTA buses get this far without the NOPD seeing them and confiscating the buses?

This violence is unbearable, the screams from the stabbings and the rapes is just too much to take at one time. Then someone discovers dead bodies in the back of the convention center. Now everyone wants to be outside, so that's where they put the bodies after raping them. They would pull the knife out, demand their bodies and when they finish slice their throats. It was a sight to see.

Outside the convention you see a chase of the NOPD and the gunmen with the sawed off shotgun in hand. Thankfully no gunshots were fired from either party. The NOPD recovered the shotgun, but the shooters were still in the convention center.

Overcrowded and at the end of the rope, people start arguing amongst themselves. Everyone wants to get out of this environment and get to normal. Normal, what's that anymore? Everything is upside down and coming to an end. I can't take it anymore, the screams, they just keep coming in my mind. Am I mentally prepared for this? Survival of the Fittest, Kill or be killed.

CHAPTER EIGHT

Fire in the Sky

FEMA I think, the military is here with some MRE. Thursday has been a day to remember, because we don't have buses but now we have food and water. The military asked us to line up for the buses, but no one moves. "We are tired of hearing the buses are coming!" exclaims one woman. The military wants us to walk all the way to the casino to get food and water. I made way to the casino for food and water. I see two people I know and wonder if some others are still alive. As I get to the food and water, I pass the news reporters that are covering the story. I thought about talking to them, but what good will that do. America never shows the whole story, only BBC. I get to the military captain that is passing out the MRE's and he tells me that I can only get 1. I said that I had 15 people or better in the group alone, what about the others. His response was that they had to make it here themselves. I tried to explain that they are tired and don't have the energy, let alone being dehydrated. I went back to the group and told them. Then I see people running at the other end. A truck with MRE's on it stopped and everyone is getting the food off of the truck. I need to get some of those and then head back to the casino, so I did. Just trying to make sure we all eat something.

Thursday night all is quiet, too quiet. The military isn't even out here tonight, I thought maybe they would patrol the area while the police rest. Then all in a sudden we hear an explosion, "They broke the levee, their trying to kill us all!!" exclaimed a herd of people. We had to cover the kids to make sure they did trample over them. BOOM, BOOM, BOOM there goes something blowing up. I hear gunshots like an AK-47 going off in between explosions. It sounds like it's coming from the Superdome and that they are blowing up Amtrack cars to cover up a shooting. I heard that they had quiet a few people that were acting up and causing confusion. Coming up in the 9th ward you tend to hear all the different guns, so I should be able to tell the difference. When I paid attention you could also hear M16's going off. Yes I have been shot at a few times, so the difference is in the sound it makes going off. With no traffic in New Orleans the sounds echo from a distance. So this is hell, I thought. I'm ready to die, I can't take any more of this. I heard the gunshots before the explosions and I heard the gunshots after the explosions.

My mind started to wander. Chris said it sounded like a helicopter crashing that was saving lives. Everyone thought that they were in danger and that the military was trying to kill them. I think no one got any sleep that night. Just after that explosion gunshots are heard right in the next block. Everyone yelling to get down. Call me hard headed but I wanted to see who was doing the shooting. I was so mad I could literally take his gun and shoot him with it. I've taken guns from people before, but I never shot anyone or even a gun for that matter. At this point I am like mad and want to curse out who ever is in charge of this whole evacuation matter. I wish I was on the rooftop of my house now, at least I wouldn't get shot at. The radio shouldn't advertise us to get to the convention center if there is no one to get us out of New Orleans. This is ridiculous, how much longer do we have to put up with this hell. Not to mention fighting off others because they are fed up. Nothing is left but a big red fire in the sky.

CHAPTER NINE
Back at it Again

Friday morning we hear screams of a woman at 5:54 in the morning. She's yelling, "Help me someone, they are stabbing me in my side, OW OW OW!!! HELP!! They are trying to kill me, can someone hear me!" I couldn't figure out where she was, I went looking as the sun came up a little, but never found her. It sounded like she was tied to the fence or wall inside a building and getting stabbed in her side. Only god knows.

7:00 a.m. everyone wakes up after a ruff night of explosions and torture, every bit of 3000 people in a frantic rush to find transportation. The parking garage across the street has 7 floors of cars and everyone was searching the building for the keys to the cars. I even went to get a 4 door car or truck to get everyone out of this, not knowing if you are going to see tomorrow you tend to do the unthinkable. I admit to searching for a car to take to Baton

Rouge, we never knew if someone was going to attack us or not and I was losing my last brain cell. My mind left me 4 days ago. I remembered about a car dealership around my old high school and started to travel there. In a frantic rage at 8 in the morning, I find out that all the cars are gone. Then again, maybe I would have been pulled over for not owning the car that I would have taken. So maybe it was for the better.

Many people started to get up and move closer to the casino where the troops were stationed at. They kept yelling that they were not going to take this anymore. What can you do? Everyone who is here to rescue seems not to know what is going on. Why would anyone want a mayor that can't control a disaster situation? Nothing against our mayor but if someone is trying to help you, that doesn't mean you don't know what you are doing. Refusing the help means you don't know what you are doing.

When I get back to my group, I find that the military listens to women more than men. 2 women out the group managed to come back with a box of Mre's, the military food, and a box of water. The military really didn't know how much of the food they were going to receive and how much food they needed to reserve. When they first got there it was 1 for everyone, now they realize we hadn't had anything to eat so they tend to be more freely.

I don't know how much more I can take of this horror. I'm seriously tired, let alone ready to go. We live in a city that has the highest tax rate I've seen and they can't take care of us when we need them. I don't know if it could get any worse than this.

The day lingers on as we hear the same old story, the buses are coming. Now we have military troops patrolling the streets. Isn't it odd that after all that shooting the night before, now we have troops on the streets. The troops claim that they are finished with the Superdome and that they don't know what is going on. They just listen to what they are told. I understand when you are not in a position of power you don't ask questions. When you are dealing with a high mass of people shouldn't you know what you are doing at all times with those people? The troops are carrying AK-47's and the safety is on, maybe this will keep the violence down.

Inside the convention center the NOPD raided the second and third floors and those that were up to no good ran out. No one got shot or killed, they just finally got a chance to have backup in case something went down. Rumors had it where the convention center seemed turned upside down. Just last night the drug users tried to burn the place down, but seems like it was fireproof because all that came out was a cloud of smoke.

Speaking of which, just on Canal st. someone set a building on fire. Knowing you don't have water pressure or a way to put it out, why would you do something like that. Someone just doesn't have anything else better to do. You can see the smoke in the sky. I saw another building on fire towards the 9th ward that looked like a warehouse.

As night falls, so do all the backup generators. Something isn't right, this don't feel good. A sudden feel of insecurity, there is no light anywhere and you can barely see the person next to you. You can see these red beams all around you, not to mention the sniper that is on the Cresent City Connection. The police prevent you from going across that bridge to get to higher ground. I thought the idea was to rescue us, not treat us like a herd and then point guns at us with infrared light. With the shooting, stabbing, yelling, screaming, crying, arguing, killing, fires, looting and most of all tired, I don't think I could take much more of this.

Then in the distance you see a woman trying to fight off a little man, yelling he raped me inside. A woman fighting back a man that raped her and no one in the crowd is even helping. No police in site and the troops are all in the buildings with the infrared beams looking for people with guns. A police car flies past us and the woman fighting the man and heads toward the casino. The woman's family asks her to leave him alone. She cries, "but he raped me, hell no he aint getting away with this." That's when I said I couldn't take anymore of this. The police car was heading back, we tried to flag him down. He wasn't slowing up, then the unlikely happens. My good friend, my roommates' other uncle, tries to stop the police car by jumping in front of it. Sigh, the car doesn't stop and he gets ran over and shot with a shotgun blast to the heart. He then lands on his back and is left for dead. No ambulance, no police, no one to help him to survive.

"That's it, I can't take this S@$# anymore, how many more people have to die!?!?!?!?!" I am in a frantic rage now. I've lost every ounce of sanity there is left. I am ready to commit suicide by going after the police man that shot him and letting the rest of the police take me out. This is ridiculous, the real criminals are still alive and an innocent man is gone. It hurts to this day to see someone you really cared for just disappear before your eyes. Everyone wanted me to calm down, I really wanted to turn the convention center right side up. I wanted justice to be served at any cost now.

The police show up with 5 cars and they see the body, they pointed those shotguns at everyone. The shotguns equipped with the flashlight so they can see what is going on at night. Now I feel like a criminal, any sudden movement and they will kill you. Remember martial law, the right to shoot to kill. Fighting sleep, I try to keep my hands up, but fear that if I fall asleep and my hands fall will they shoot me. My mind is racing and I can't think at all. The next thing I remember was falling asleep finally. I know that tomorrow I'll be right back at it again.

CHAPTER TEN
Day of Rejoice

When I woke the next morning, Saturday, I realize it wasn't a dream and all this tragedy really happened. I am really fed up and now I am going to the reporters, someone who will listen, the BBC. I made my way up to the casino where everything seemed to be. Why didn't we just come up here with all the elderly in the first place? The thought never crossed our minds. I ran across an old co-worker of mine and he said that my old father in law was at the casino steps. Everything was going ok for him and I wished him the best of luck.

I get to the news crew and said I have a story for you. In a state of mind of wanting to get the hell out of here I asked if they were interested. "Sure, what you got?" they say. So they turn the camera on and I tell them that there is a dead body of a good friend of mine in the middle of the street. "What happened?" they ask. I let them know that he got shot and killed, and ask them in return, "How many more people have to die before we get out of here?" They loved to hear that, they finally got a good story to tell. They ask, "Would you mind if we go see the body of your friend?" I said, "If you go down there, out of respect of the family, would you not get closer than 1 block away?" They said, "Sure." I let them know I didn't have power or authority to give that information, but to ask the family if they could release any information.

I make way to the casino in search of my old father. I was married at one point, but got a divorce. I found him at the steps of the casino looking pretty good. We sat and talked about the past few days and how he heard everything, but I seemed to be in the heart of it all. We try to exchange numbers but without a pen or a cell phone it was kinda hard. I told him to let my daughters know I was alive and that I'll see them again someday. He made it out ok.

I travel back to the group and everyone is packing. "What's going on?" I ask. They say that the buses are lined up a couple of streets over. Chris already took off in search of the buses. The group that we had kinda split up, at this point I think everyone just wanted to get on the bus. We gather everything together and search for the buses before everyone realized that the buses were here. "Is everyone with us?" I ask as we find the buses just loading up people 10 at a time in 5 different locations. Thank God that it is finally over, so we thought. It might be over for the convention center, but it was just a day to rejoice.

CHAPTER ELEVEN

The Long Ride

As we get on the bus the first thing I want to do is use the bathroom and go to sleep. I found a seat and asked if anyone had a Tylenol p.m. so I could definitely sleep. They told me I was sleep for like 4 hours. It felt good to finally sleep and wake up to a different environment. As we approach the outskirts of Baton Rouge, we see the two RTA buses that were stolen in a parking lot. I think to myself, "It feels good to be on dry land." Little did I know we were going on a journey where we didn't know our destination. I really didn't care at this point, anything was better than New Orleans right now.

We headed for Houston, but as we got to the border of Texas, the police directed us to go to Shreveport. They were saying that Houston and Dallas were already over-crowded, so the bus driver headed north to get to Shreveport. We approach Shreveport and the police there asked for the person who gave the permission to come here. The state police man didn't escort us to Shreveport and the police there said that we should go to Alexandria. Now what, we are on this bus for 24 hours already and we don't know where we are going. We traveled the southwest Louisiana, then the northwest Louisiana and now we are going northeast. Are we ever going to get out of Louisiana? So we finally stop to get something to eat, ahhhh some real food. At that point the state troopers finally got someone to escort us to a destination, Arkansas, at an army base.

I fall asleep on the journey to Arkansas and I know it took another 12 hours to get to the destination which I think was north Arkansas. When we finally get there it is chaotic and no organization. I don't think I'll be here long at all. I am just glad we are over the long ride.

CHAPTER TWELVE

A Base in Ruin

As we get off the bus and stretch our legs, we are in a long line of buses. The line of buses is over 3 miles long, the base is longer. There must be at least 12,000 refugees here that are trying to live. The first thing on my mind is a shot for being in that nasty water. I also needed my medication, because my leg wasn't doing too good. I got all that taken care of as soon as we got registered at the base. I told everyone that it wouldn't be a good idea to stay here because of the fact of waiting 2 hours in a line just for a meal. Something had to change and it was. God said, ask and you shall receive. So after I took my medicine, I asked for a different place to stay. In the distance I see an odd looking bus, different from the evacuation buses. I ask around to see what the bus was doing here. People were telling me that a church in Alma Arkansas was taking people in that wanted to be in a church. The maximum was 60 people, I immediately ran back to the group to tell them. I said, "It would be a good idea to be in a church because of the fact that this place was over crowded." It took all day just to get everything together for everyone. With everyone having their mind lost that was in the group, the last thing they needed was to be around a whole bunch of people that really didn't care about their environment. I heard people saying that they have 15 people per housing and that it didn't matter what the ratio was of men to women. One woman said, "How do they expect me to stay with 13 men and another woman? How do they know if those men aren't going to try to rape me? I'm not staying there like that, oh no not me!!" I don't blame her, it seems the whole base is in ruin.

CHAPTER THIRTEEN
Helping Hands

After we got on the bus to go to the church, it wasn't packed at all. Seems like they only had 30 people on the bus, I guess people have a problem with church. We travel for about 45 minutes to Alma Arkansas and reach the church with no problem. As we get inside they ask us to register with them, so that FEMA knows where we are. The next thing they ask is if we got our shots or if we need medication. They did in fact get my medicine for my leg as an emergency prescription. Anything you wanted they got it for you, an air mattress for a bed instead of hard concrete. Food without a line to stand in, drinks, oh man all the coke, pepsi, water, juice and the endless snacks. I felt like I was in heaven, no lie. These people I thank with all my heart for doing what they did for us there. I just didn't want to leave, I felt that there were still some good people out there in the world. Thank you Jesus for guiding me to these people who helped me get back on my feet.

Then people were coming to them with donations for the hurricane victims. Just so happens that a man is exactly like me in size, where did he come from? He had shoes my size, pants my size, shirts my size and most of all he had a bible my size. I like to see what I am reading and he had this huge bible that had pictures of what happened. Most people that read this book may not be religious, but you have to admit, it had to be God who sent this man to me on this day. He could have come when I was gone.

The man asks if I needed a suitcase, oh yeah! Now I can put the shirts and pants in the suitcase and not worry if they are going to get ruined. I get back inside and tell everyone about the church having a second building with clothing donations if they wanted to look. They found books they wanted, clothes that fit and most of all a piece of mind.

My roommate's family came from Mississippi to come and get us to live with family instead of having no direction. That night we have service at the church, and most of all I remember a phrase. The phrase was, "Leave it at the alter." So I did, I left my friends death at the alter and asked for God to let him Rest In Peace. Rest in Peace my brother, for you are the only man I let call me Honky. They do still have people that care about Americans' in their own country.

The rest is history. Questions only remain, but will they be answered. The mayor is up for re-election soon, will he make it? The president will try for another term, will he make it? The governor, will she make it? The way they handled this disaster, I don't think so. Someone out of the three should have taken control of the situation instead of what happened. I leave it in god's hands, the only true helping hands.

ACKNOWLEDGMENTS

First off I would like to thank God for letting me live. I can't thank him enough, because I could count many, many times I could have died. With the water as high as it was, if I didn't know how to swim I wouldn't have made it. The killing that was going on at the convention center, I wouldn't have survived that. Not without God protecting us. We just had to be strong and believe that we are going to be alright. Now we see, we are all alright.

I would like to thank the mother I never had, she knows who she is. Without her holding on I don't think I would have held on as long as I did. I fell apart after her brother's death but she told me, "I got this." So I let her handle the situation. Thank you for everything you have done for me before, during and after this hurricane. That's why you are the mother I never had.

Thanks to Charles. You have taught me so much about myself and the direction that I should be going in. Without you and the experience we went through I would be the person I am today. Thanks

Thanks to my boy Chris. Man if you weren't by my side in this tragedy I don't think I would have made it saving those people alone. It was hard at times, and I did need you and I thank you for what you have done. You went above and beyond what you had to.

Thanks to my roommates' brother, g keep ya head up ya heard. You gonna make it big, just keep going. Thanks

Thanks to crazy uncle, man without the fun times we had after the hurricane I don't think I would be sane. I think I would be in a mental hospital, it's always the fun times that take your mind off of things.

Thanks to all that helped get me where I am today, you all know who you are. Keep It Real. Much love. One.

Steve M. Banka

ABOUT THE AUTHOR

The author of this book, Steve Banka, is a white male that grew up in a black city. Growing up in the 9th ward of New Orleans was as ruff as it gets. Struggling all his life to prove himself over and over again, he always strives to help those in need. Although he wasn't welcome in many places, alot of people remember him as, "The only white boy to help them out." Father of 2 children and divorced from a black woman, he always felt that he didn't fit in. Now the only thing he wants is to be with his children again, like a family, the family he never had.

www.ingramcontent.com/pod-product-compliance
Lightning Source LLC
Chambersburg PA
CBHW021250280526
45784CB00005B/2312